Date: 8/3/12

DISCOVERING CRABS

Lorijo Metz

PowerKiDS
press

New York

To Jay, Jim, both Johns, Bill, both Larrys, and all the other crabs at Caribou

Published in 2012 by The Rosen Publishing Group, Inc.
29 East 21st Street, New York, NY 10010

First Edition

Editor: Amelie von Zumbusch
Book Design: Kate Laczynski

Photo Credits: Cover © www.iStockphoto.com/Constantine Dimizas; p. 4 Ben Cranke/Getty Images; pp. 5, 7, 10–11, 13 (bottom) Shutterstock.com; pp. 6, 8, 18, 19 iStockphoto/Thinkstock; p. 9 (top) Rosemary Calvert/Getty Images; p. 9 (bottom) Jeff Foott/Getty Images; p. 12 © www.iStockphoto.com/Sandy Franz; p. 13 (top) Paul Souders/Getty Images; p. 14 Reinhard Dirscherl/Getty Images; p. 15 David Liittschwager/Getty Images; p. 16 Heinrich van den Berg/Getty Images; p. 17 Norbert Wu/Getty Images; p. 20 © www.iStockphoto.com/pamspix; p. 21 © www.iStockphoto.com/Aimin Tang; p. 22 Hemera/Thinkstock.

Library of Congress Cataloging-in-Publication Data

Metz, Lorijo.
 Discovering crabs / by Lorijo Metz. — 1st ed.
    p. cm. — (Along the shore)
 Includes index.
 ISBN 978-1-4488-4993-2 (library binding)
 1. Crabs—Juvenile literature. I. Title.
 QL444.M33M48 2012
 595.3'86—dc22

                              2011000153

Manufactured in the United States of America

CPSIA Compliance Information: Batch #WS11PK: For Further Information contact Rosen Publishing, New York, New York at 1-800-237-9932

CONTENTS

INSIDE OUT AND SIDEWAYS

What animal breathes like a fish yet can live on land, has no bones inside its body, and runs sideways not forward? If you guessed a crab, you are right! Crabs are interesting animals. Most crabs live in the ocean, in **salt water**. Over time, many **adapted**, or became used, to living in **freshwater**, such as lakes and rivers. Still others adapted to living on land.

Fiddler crabs, such as this one, often live on beaches. They also live in other kinds of land along the shore, such as salt marshes or mangrove forests.

This is a Halloween crab. Halloween crabs are land crabs. They are also known as moon crabs, mouthless crabs, and harlequin land crabs.

Crabs, like lobsters and shrimp, belong to a class of animals called **crustaceans**. Crustaceans do not have skeletons, or bones, inside their bodies. They have hard outer shells, called **exoskeletons**. Exoskeletons keep their soft bodies inside safe.

LOTS OF LEGS

Crabs have wide bodies with 10 legs growing out of them. Like your legs, crab legs are jointed. This lets them bend. Crabs use eight legs for walking. In some **species**, or kinds, of crabs, the back pair is used for swimming or digging. A crab's two front legs have powerful claws that look like big pliers. Crabs use them to catch food and scare off enemies.

You can see all 10 of this crab's legs in this picture. You can see the claws on the front pair of legs, too.

Some crabs, such as the one shown here, have one claw that is larger and another claw that is smaller.

CRAB FACT

Crabs walk sideways because their knees bend sideways. It is easier and faster for them to walk this way.

Like fish, crabs use **gills** to breathe. However, crabs can breathe outside of water, as well as under it. Gills must be wet to work. On land, crabs have special ways to keep their gills from drying out.

SO MANY KINDS OF CRABS

There are more than 4,500 species of crabs. They come in many sizes. Emerald crabs are about the size of your big toe. Dungeness crabs can grow to be more than 10 inches (25 cm) wide. Dungeness crabs are found from California to Alaska. They are prized for their meat.

Crabs can be very colorful. Sally Lightfoot crabs come in many colors, from spotted brown to

Blue land crabs, such as this one, are also called giant land crabs. They are different colors at different stages of their lives.

bright red, yellow, and blue. They are a common sight for visitors to the Galápagos Islands.

Different kinds of crabs live in different places. For example, mangrove land crabs live under mangrove trees on the beaches along the Caribbean Sea.

There are more than 90 kinds of fiddler crabs. They got their name because the males sometimes look as though they are playing fiddles when they move their claws.

JAPANESE SPIDER CRABS

The Japanese spider crab's legs are so long that this crab could step over a car! Japanese spider crabs are almost all legs. From the tip of one claw to the other, they can grow to be up to 13 feet (4 m) long. Their bodies are only a small part of this, measuring

Japanese spider crabs eat shellfish. They also eat the bodies of sea animals that have fallen to the ocean floor.

CRAB FACT

One of the largest living Japanese spider crabs ever caught lives in the Sea Life Aquarium in Blankenberge, Belgium. Its name is Crabzilla. It is more than 10 feet (3 m) long.

15 inches (38 cm) or less. Though they look huge, these crabs do not weigh very much.

While Japanese spider crabs may look like monsters, they are really very gentle. They are found deep in the Pacific Ocean near Japan. Many live as deep as 1,000 feet (305 m) down. They can live for nearly 100 years.

BLUE CRABS

Steamed blue crabs are a favorite dish for people living along the Atlantic coast. People like to eat blue crabs because their meat is sweet.

Male blue crabs have bright blue claws and legs. People often say they are beautiful swimmers. The females have bright orange tips on their claws that make it look as if they have painted nails. While all crabs can run sideways, blue crabs also swim sideways.

Blue crabs are good swimmers. Their back legs are wide. The crabs use these wide legs to paddle through the water.

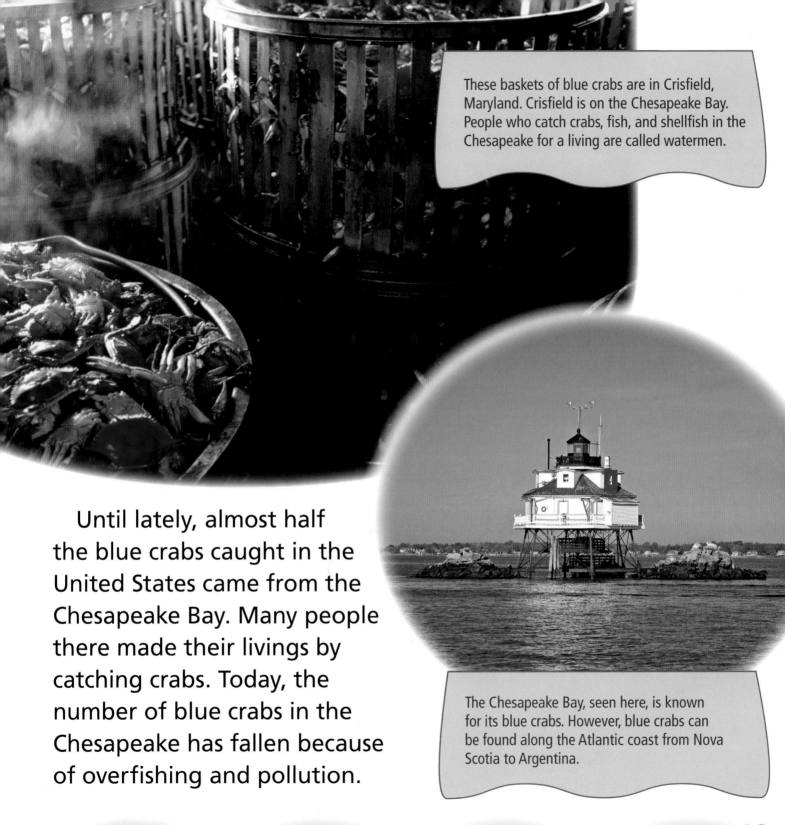

These baskets of blue crabs are in Crisfield, Maryland. Crisfield is on the Chesapeake Bay. People who catch crabs, fish, and shellfish in the Chesapeake for a living are called watermen.

Until lately, almost half the blue crabs caught in the United States came from the Chesapeake Bay. Many people there made their livings by catching crabs. Today, the number of blue crabs in the Chesapeake has fallen because of overfishing and pollution.

The Chesapeake Bay, seen here, is known for its blue crabs. However, blue crabs can be found along the Atlantic coast from Nova Scotia to Argentina.

BABY CRABS AND MOLTING

Female crabs may lay thousands, even millions, of eggs at a time. They carry the eggs under their stomachs until they are ready to **hatch**, or break open. The baby crabs that come out of the eggs are called **larvae**. Once hatched, larvae are on their own. It may take as long as a month for them to grow shells.

If you look closely, you can see the eggs that this female crab is carrying on the underside of her body.

This is a crab larva. While a group of newly hatched crabs are called larvae, one on its own is called a larva. Larvae go through several stages as they grow.

To grow, crabs must **molt**. This means they grow new, larger shells under their old ones. When their old shells break, crabs climb out of them. After a few hours, their new shells harden. Young crabs molt often. Older crabs molt only once or twice a year.

WHAT DO CRABS EAT?

Most crabs rest by day and hunt at night. This way they stay safely out of sight of birds and other animals that hunt them. Crabs will eat bits of whatever lands on the ocean floor. This includes dead fish and plants. Some species of crabs have strong claws they use to open the shells of oysters and other crustaceans, including

Many kinds of crabs will eat whatever food they can catch. This crab is eating a blue bottle fly.

other crabs. Some crabs have thin claws with sharp, pointed edges, perfect for catching fish.

Crabs that live on land may eat worms and insects. Crabs that live along rivers and lakes dine on fish eggs, frogs, and water plants.

WHICH ANIMALS EAT CRABS?

Many animals eat crabs. Seagulls, octopuses, and other crabs consider them food. Larvae are easy **prey**, or food, for fish. Crabs are in the greatest danger when they are molting and their new shells are still soft.

Luckily, crabs are good at hiding. Some crabs have coloring that helps them hide. Harlequin crabs have colorful spots, which help them blend

The sea otter is another animal that eats crabs. Sea otters live along the coasts of the northern part of the Pacific Ocean.

This seagull is eating a crab. Crabs are an important food for many animals that live along the shore.

in with their surroundings. Other crabs move fast. Ghost crabs run so fast they seem to disappear. Crabs also have special ways of keeping watch for animals that want to eat them. Their tiny eyes are on the ends of **eyestalks**. Crabs can turn their eyestalks so they can see in all directions. They can also pull them inside their shells.

CRAB FACT

Crabs do not always hide. They also fight their enemies. In a fight, their strong claws come in handy. If a crab loses a claw or leg while fighting, it will grow back in time.

CRABS AND PEOPLE

People who fish for crabs are called crabbers. There are several ways to catch crabs. Today, most crabbers use crab pots. Crab pots are special cagelike traps filled with fish or other meat. Crabbers must be careful when handling crabs. Crab claws are strong and sharp.

There are many ways to eat crab. Deep-fried, in soups,

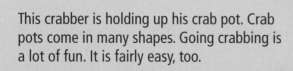

This crabber is holding up his crab pot. Crab pots come in many shapes. Going crabbing is a lot of fun. It is fairly easy, too.

This crab pot is full of Dungeness crabs. Dungeness crabs live along the west coast of North America. They are considered one of the tastiest kinds of crabs.

and in salads are just a few. People generally remove crabmeat from the shell before eating it. When eating soft-shell crabs, though, people eat the whole crab. Soft-shell crabs are crabs caught just as they finish molting. This means their new shells are still soft.

CRABS AND YOU

To make sure crab **populations**, or numbers, remain healthy, people have taken steps to control crab fishing. However, pollution also causes trouble in the underwater world of crabs. This also makes problems for people and many other animals that depend on crabs for food.

If you visit a beach, be on the lookout for crabs. Always be careful if you pick up a crab. Remember, they can pinch you!

To find out more about crabs, visit your local zoo or aquarium. If you learn how to care for them, crabs make interesting pets. Your librarian or local pet shop owner can help you learn more.

GLOSSARY

adapted (uh-DAPT-ed) Changed to fit new conditions.

crustaceans (krus-TAY-shunz) Animals that have no backbones, have hard shells and other body parts, and live mostly in water.

exoskeletons (ek-soh-SKEH-leh-tunz) The hard coverings on the outside of animals' bodies that hold and guard the soft insides.

eyestalks (EYE-stawks) Body parts that hold up eyes.

freshwater (FRESH-wah-ter) Water without salt.

gills (GILZ) Body parts that fish and other animals use for breathing.

hatch (HACH) To come out of an egg.

larvae (LAHR-vee) Animals in an early period of life.

molt (MOHLT) To shed hair, feathers, shell, horns, or skin.

populations (pop-yoo-LAY-shunz) Groups of animals or people living in the same place.

prey (PRAY) An animal that is hunted by another animal for food.

salt water (SAWLT WAW-ter) Water, such as the ocean, that has salt in it.

species (SPEE-sheez) One kind of living thing. All people are one species.

INDEX

WEB SITES

Due to the changing nature of Internet links, PowerKids Press has developed an online list of Web sites related to the subject of this book. This site is updated regularly. Please use this link to access the list:

www.powerkidslinks.com/alsh/crabs/